Collage of Poetry

Oxana Tatarenko

BookLeaf Publishing

India | USA | UK

Presentation by *BookLeaf Publishing*

Web: www.bookleafpub.com

E-mail: info@bookleafpub.com

ISBN: 9789357215244

First edition 2023

DEDICATION

To those who still love poetry, who use it to overcome hurdles of life and relationships. To the ones that find love in writing and live in reading.

ACKNOWLEDGEMENT

To those who dare to dream, dare to imagine ...
to those who are the visionaries and persuers.

PREFACE

I write poetry because there is something beautiful in a tiny little paragraph that can summarize everything a person can feel. Poetry is not only a written form of expression of love, but also pain and other emotions. It is a well written word or a sentence with all the words you weren't sure how to convey a message to another. Poetry is one of my artistic expressions and most of these poems are written in the time of my healing while others just came to me.

Little angel

Your little Angel is all grown up
She haunts the halls here every night
With loud moans and groaning sounds
She drags a body on the ground
With screams and wails heard for miles
When it's all been said and done she comes back
to claim another one.

Undying love

I want a love that will not break
With every bated breath you take
I want it to withstand the time
I want it to be forever mine

Happiness

3

Scorching tears run down her face
Washing her happiness without a trace
Right as she thought she couldn't be happy
again. Happiness found its way In.

Leaving

When the hardest thing you thought
Would be,
Leaving the one you loved so easily,
Alas, you overcame the biggest hurdle of the
pain.
You spend a night without them, and then a
week, a month, a year.

Hard work

5

She worked hard on the
Relationship she thought she wanted
Just not the one she truly deserved.

Numb

She felt so much in her marriage that in that time
she learned; the feelings she had felt,
And how she wasn't heard, and she was lonely
and sad sometimes. Something broke inside of
her, she thought it was her soul or maybe heart
or both.
The numbness filled the ache inside,
The ache of being free and happy which no
longer had applied. She wanted to be free and
careless to let herself just be ... Herself, but then
numbness spread throughout and her body felt
like a foe that betrayed her everywhere she'd go.

No Escape

You can't escape your past. You can try to forget it, but memories are tough they are like a haunting spirit. They'll haunt you, specially when you're down.

Her love

Her love is like a jungle, so beautiful and vast. There are parts in the jungle which are not for human eyes. The darkness that resides there is empty, cold and void... but that is where I stay and where I thrive.

Love

I surrender myself whole, with no expectations. I let go of fear and reservations, I let all go of any preconceived notions, of what love must be. I'm done daydreaming of love that is greater than any love, I'm going to live the love I want now, because I will love myself without a drop of doubt.

Morning

The sun had risen scattering ambers in its wake,
lighting up the flames all through sky.
The marvel of the first light.
As the East were already hard at work, the west
still sleeping …
And all those in between commuting to and fro

Damaged

He was a tall man with beautiful eyes he looked
as though he could touch the skies.
He had an aura about him of confidence and
courage. But no one knew on the inside that he
was damaged.

Warmer days

I always long for summer days,
On the darkest winter nights,
Though I appreciate today,
But thoughts are drifting to summer
I love the winter with all its beauty
Eventually it all becomes so tiresome.

Darkness

I lay in bed as if I'm dead,
Motionless, my eyes look around the room
And all I see is emptiness and doom.
With a blink of an eye the darkness surrounds
me, I start to feel it inside me.
I become numb, but when the lights go on
I feel alive, I can finally breathe like you are
with me.
Until the lights go out and then,
The darkness moves right in and consumes me
from within.
Like a parasite it moving closer and closer,
Into my body and through my veins up into my
heart.
And once it swallows me whole, I feel emptier
than before.
An empty shell and empty vessel
Moving through life with no purpose or
direction.

Her wants

All she wanted was love,
The security and care
Caress of beautiful soft words
About her soul and mind
Her values and morals
Her smarts and wise comments
She was ready to receive
Just like a beautiful lotus bud
All she needed was a gentle nudge
To open her up and make her bloom
So she can float in the open waters of love

Silence

15

I sit in silence
I find comfort in it
I can think and plan
So many thoughts race through my mind
So I am still, I hear my breathing
My heart is beating pretty loud
I find comfort in this silence,
it helps me love more.

Letting go

I love him but I had to let him go
He wasn't good for me, you know?!
It was so difficult to love him too
It's hard to love a person who offers
No comfort, No security within.
And nothing to help you hold on.
And yet this was the most painful thing I had
done.

Dreams

The dreams I have are so unique
One day I'm on the beach
Another In a castle's library
One day I'm on an island
Another in an underground hell
But only one thing is the same
I have to save myself.

Shadows

It is the coldest night of the year,
The snow is falling flurries are landing
and melting right away
Candles are lit and on the wall
You see a Bunch of shadows fall,
Making shapes of different sizes as
They dance against the wall.

Ocean

19

The ocean is blue and deep
There is no telling what's in it
No one goes to the deepest end
No one can survive there
The ocean is vast and big there're so many
secrets it likes to keep.

Stars

The sky is dark and in the city you cannot see
any of the stars
But it is dark beyond that city and all the stars
are shining bright.
They sparkle, flash and twinkle
Some pulse and jiggle in the sky
While others glow and some fall from above.